PUTTING ON YOUR FACE

PUTTING ON YOUR FACE

The Ultimate Guide to Cosmetics

by Zia Wesley-Hosford

BANTAM BOOKS
TORONTO · NEW YORK · LONDON · SYDNEY · AUCKLAND

PUTTING ON YOUR FACE: THE ULTIMATE GUIDE TO COSMETICS
A Bantam Book / February 1985

Illustration from Being Beautiful by Zia Wesley-Hosford. Copyright © 1983 by Zia Wesley-Hosford. Illustrated by Nia Cabrerra. Reprinted by permission of Whatever Publishing, Inc., Mill Valley, California.

Library of Congress Cataloging in Publication Data

Wesley-Hosford, Zia.
    Putting on your face.

    1. Beauty, Personal.   2. Women—Health and hygiene.
3. Skin—Care and hygiene.   4. Cosmetics.   I. Title.
RA778.W247   1985   646.7'042   84-18583
ISBN 0-553-34141-3 (U.S.: pbk.)

Published simultaneously in the United States and Canada

PRINTED IN THE UNITED STATES OF AMERICA

S   0 9 8 7 6 5 4 3 2 1

Contents

Introduction

Before you begin to read this book there is something very important that I want you to know, and that is: Don't be concerned if you've never read or heard most of this information before. The skin-care information you've probably received over the years has come mostly from fashion magazines. Though these magazines are great for a lot of things, they're supported by cosmetic manufacturers, so you can see how they might tend to be just the teeniest bit biased. The truth is that the information these magazines print has one purpose only and that is to sell products.

Personally, I have nothing against buying cosmetics; in fact, I strongly recommend them because the proper ones can and do make a difference. However, up until now, women have had no way of knowing which products are good or bad, short of buying and trying them. At one time or another we've all spent some outrageous sum of money on some "wonder" cream that not only didn't do what it promised, but actually caused skin problems. To make matters worse, every season cosmetic companies come out with "new improved" creams and lotions which, more often than not, are just newly-packaged versions of the same old stuff. No wonder women tell me that they're feeling ripped off and confused. Where can they turn?

If you've ever asked a saleswoman for product information, you know she'll give nothing but glowing reports of the miraculous powers of her line. How could she do anything else? Who would buy anything from her if she said, "This cream is just Vaseline with a dozen chemicals and some perfume." And using price to determine quality doesn't work either. Some of the most expensive cosmetics are made with the cheapest ingredients. Most of the time what we're paying for are fancy packages and million-dollar ad campaigns. But *Putting on Your Face* will take you out of the confusion and into true product and skin-care knowledge. In Part One of this book, you will learn how to determine your skin type accurately. For years cosmetic companies have been brainwashing American women into believing that their skin is "dry, dry, dry . . . dry as the desert floor." What they're really doing is trying to sell, sell, sell hundreds of varieties of moisturizers, night creams, rejuvenation tonics, and so on. Knowing your true skin type will not only protect your skin, but will also protect you from media hype.

In Part Two, you will be instructed in a simple, effective daily program for maintaining healthy, youthful skin. In addition, explanations of the various types of skin-care products, from cleansers to exfoliating masks, are provided to help you decipher any cosmetic label. Why not be able to understand cosmetics as well as you understand food? After all, it wasn't until several years ago that consumers began reading labels on food packages. The result has been higher quality food products with fewer (or no) chemicals and artificial ingredients. With the growing concern about what we put *in* our bodies, why should we care any less about what we put *on* our bodies? If women refuse to throw money away on inferior products, cosmetic manufacturers will be forced to make improvements, and we will all benefit. The product recommendations section will help you to choose readily available quality skin-care products, specifically designed for your skin type.

Part Three discusses the problem of breakouts, and takes a look at what causes blemishes on the skin and how to solve these problems.

Finally, Part Four guides you in your selection of cosmetics, from blusher to eye shadow.

I was asked to write this book because I've taught hundreds of men and women how to clear up facial problems and flaws quickly and simply. But it's important to remember, as you read, that this is the first time you may be hearing these things. If they seem a little strange, that's to be expected.

For example, contrary to what cosmetic companies would have us believe, the real secret to beautiful, healthy skin lies in keeping it *TAUT.* This means maintaining the skin on the tight-dry side, rather than softening it to slackness with creams.

When you use the products and procedures recommended here, you'll see an immediate difference. You'll notice that your face will feel dry. This may be the most important change for you, so I want to explain it. Many skin problems, like acne, whiteheads, blackheads, dehydration, excessive oiliness, and loss of elasticity can be directly related to the use of heavy, mineral oil-based cosmetics, specifically moisturizers, "milky cleansers," and foundations. When I take women off these products and replace them with natural oil or water-based products, problems clear up almost overnight.

So, as you begin your new skin-care program and your face feels *tight,* remember that's just how you want it to feel. To assure yourself that what you're feeling is in fact tight but not dry, look in the mirror. If the skin looks smooth, even a bit shiny, that's good. If it looks chalky, dull, or flaky, that's dry—and we'll take care of that too. But the *feeling* of tightness will be the same in both cases.

In a very short time, you'll learn to love that feeling, especially when your face looks better than it ever has!

Part One

WHAT TYPE
OF SKIN
DO YOU HAVE?

Common Misconceptions and Complaints About Skin

Before we begin, let me clarify some common misconceptions and complaints about skin type.

Breaking out means there is excessive oil in that area.

Breakouts can be caused by oiliness but this isn't the only cause. Stress, cosmetic allergy, improper cleansing, poor elimination, toxic reaction, food allergy, and hormonal imbalance due to menstruation, birth control pills, or puberty can also be responsible for blemishes.

My skin gets oily halfway through the day.

The three major causes of oily-looking skin are:

1. The use of an oil-based "milky cleanser" that is tissued off.
2. The use of an oil-based makeup base.
3. The use of a moisturizer.

These products leave a coating of mineral oil on the skin's surface.

I have dryness around my nose—it's always peeling and red.

This condition is caused by use of an astringent that is too strong for the skin type, or just too strong.

I have dryness around my eyes.

Everyone has dryness around the eyes because there are no oil glands there. It's also important to know that the skin around the eyes is the thinnest skin on the entire body. This makes the eye area very delicate.

My forehead is excessively oily so I'm always breaking out there.

Very often, women with this complaint wear bangs. The oil from the hair causes the breakouts.

My chin gets oily sometimes, and breaks out.

Once again, this isn't always oil. Very often it's stress. The area on the face that breaks out from stress is along the jawline and onto the chin. The habit of cupping the chin in the palm of the hand to lean on is another cause for breakouts here.

I'm oily on my nose and forehead and dry everywhere else.

Usually people who are oily in one area are *normal* in other areas, rather than dry.

My skin is very oily so I use a facial scrub to wash with, twice a day.

Using a facial scrub, like "cleansing grains" or "honey and almond" removes dead skin cells which allows deeper cleansing. In the process these products also activate oil glands. So using these on a daily basis will actually magnify the very problem you're trying to solve. These products should be used once or twice weekly to slough off the dead outer layer of cells and deep-clean the pores.

I use Clearasil (or Stridex pads) daily to prevent breakouts.

Products like these are designed to be used on pimples or white-heads to dry them out. Using them on healthy skin will *really* dry it out.

After I wash my face it feels like it's going to crack. I have to put on a moisturizer.

This is an indication that the product being used for cleansing is too harsh. The face should feel tight, not dry. If it looks smooth, that's tight. If it looks chalky, dull, and/or flaky, that's dry. Drying out the face, then putting on a moisturizer to rectify it has become a common vicious cycle.

I don't wear makeup because it clogs pores.

Mineral oil-based makeup does clog pores, unless you have truly dry skin. However, water-based foundation will actually protect the skin by acting as a barrier to pollutants and absorbing oil as it is secreted during the day.

How and Why
Skin Changes

The body changes which occur during puberty bring about the first noticeable change in skin. The increase in hormones affects emotions as well as oil glands, and acne or breakouts are common. The best way to deal with this change is to "calm down" the skin. This means using cleansing products that are gentle, mild, and/or medicated. This is also a good time to begin vitamin/mineral supplements, and to clean up the diet. Preservatives, artificial colorings and flavorings, caffeine, and refined sugars can add to skin problems by creating even more imbalance in the body.

The second body change which affects the skin usually occurs around age 25. This is actually a metabolic change in which the metabolism slows down. Very often, overactive oil glands will slow down as well, so oily skin may become combination skin.

Somewhere between the ages of 30 and 35, women usually notice an even greater change: dehydration. This is, in part, one of the results of decreased oil production. It may also be the result of years spent in the sun, of smoking cigarettes, drinking alcohol, or drinking caffeine. It seems as if we can get away with all kinds of excesses in our twenties, but not after 30.

Dehydration gives the skin a dry or "papery" look and it loses its natural glow. Fine lines are also more visible on dehydrated skin. Once again, appropriate skin-care products as well as proper diet and nutritional supplements are vital.

Around the age of 50, oil and sweat glands decrease production even more. It now becomes absolutely necessary to help the skin retain moisture.

In my first book, *Being Beautiful,* I address, in depth, the subject of vitamins as they relate to skin. However, to get advice that is tailored to you personally, you may want to consult a nutritionist.

Another effect of age on the skin is the breakdown of collagen, a natural protein that holds the skin together. Dr. Alan Gaynor, a cosmetic dermatologist from San Francisco and an expert in the use of collagen implantation, describes this protein as "a microscopic network of fibers, woven together like threads in a fabric." Repetitive expressions, such as smiling, frowning, and squinting eventually cause the collagen to weaken and break down. Other factors that contribute to the breakdown of collagen are sun exposure and pulling and rubbing the skin. As a result, the skin begins to lose its shape and resiliency; lines, wrinkles, and other signs of age begin to appear.

Lately we've been inundated with hundreds of cosmetics containing collagen. Unfortunately, no one has ever proven that collagen penetrates the skin when applied topically. But the good news is that dermatologists are getting incredibly good results reversing the signs of age—lines and wrinkles—with collagen injections. Because it is a natural, living substance, already present in the skin, it is assimilated and becomes part of the area into which it has been injected.

To the best of my knowledge, the only treatments which actually erase lines and wrinkles are plastic surgery and collagen injections. In some cases, facial isometric exercises, acupressure, or acupuncture "facelifts" also can be effective.

Because of the various changes which affect skin, it is important to analyze your skin type correctly every few years. The one thing you can count on, however, is that skin becomes drier with age.

Why You Need
to Know
Your Skin Type

In order to have beautiful skin you have to know your skin type. The four basic skin types are: oily, dry, combination, and normal. A fifth category is one called "aging," which can be either normal, combination, or dry, but must be treated with additional care.

Oily skin produces too much oil. It can be balanced, to an extent, internally as well as externally. One advantage of oily skin is that it ages more slowly than normal or dry skin.

Internal: Cut down on excessive oil and fat in the diet. Dairy products have an adverse effect on oily skin because of their high fat content.

External: Discontinue use of all oil-based cosmetics.

Dry Skin has a dull, chalky appearance and may actually flake off if gently scraped with a fingernail. It suffers from either inadequate production of oil or dehydration (robbed of moisture).

Internal: Avoid improper nutrition, such as radical diets which eliminate all oils or all protein. Be aware of insufficient water intake, and excessive amounts of alcohol, cigarettes, drugs, and caffeine.

External: Discontinue use of harsh soaps or cleansers and/or astringents that are either too strong or not needed. Avoid moisturizers containing mineral oil. Do not use excessively (more than twice a week) exfoliating creams, masks, or scrubs.

Combination Skin, as its name implies, is partially dry or normal and partially oily. This skin type is usually oily in the "T-Zone," the area across the forehead, down the nose, and sometimes onto the chin. This is the most common skin type.

Normal Skin has no areas of excessive oiliness or dryness. There may be slight oiliness somewhere in the "T-Zone," but never excessive. Normal skin is basically balanced throughout.

Aging Skin can begin any time after 35 years old, but is usually not apparent until sometime after 40. The aging signs we notice first are superficial (tiny) lines, expression lines, loss of elasticity, slackness of the skin around the eyes, and a dull look to the skin.

How to Determine
Your True Skin Type

To get a true skin-type analysis, you'll need to purchase a bar of mild, nondrying soap. Choose one from the list below:

- Cooper Laboratory's Aveenobar (soap-free)
- Estée Lauder's Basic Cleansing Bar
- Ortho Pharmaceutical's Purpose
- Pierre Cattier's Nature de France (five different bars, each designed for different skin types)
- Steifel Laboratory's Oilatum
- Westwood Pharmaceutical's Lowila (soap-free)

All of these soaps can be found in pharmacies, with the exception of Pierre Cattier's, which is carried in health food stores, and Lauder's, which can be found in major department stores.

I don't recommend deodorant and perfumed soaps because they are very drying. I refer to these soaps as "harsh," because along with dehydration they destroy the natural pH balance of the skin. This temporarily destroys the "acid mantle," an amazing protective mechanism that acts like an invisible shield by maintaining the skin at a pH of between 4.5 and 5.5. You may have seen the phrases "pH balanced" or "low pH" on cosmetic labels. The initials stand for "potential Hydrogen." The pH scale is a way of categorizing substances into acids or alkalines. Citrus is acid;

baking soda is alkaline. The scale goes from 0 to 14 with acids at the low end and alkalines at the top. Cleansers or soaps having a pH that matches that of the skin will not disturb the acid mantle. Fortunately, even if we do destroy this invisible shield, the body will automatically set it up again in about three hours. But why be unprotected for those hours?

After you have chosen a soap for your skin-type analysis, follow these directions:

1. Wash your face with a mild, nondrying soap as discussed on page 13. Rinse well (20-30 splashes with clean, comfortably hot water), then pat dry.
2. **Don't put anything on your face following the washing.**
3. Wait two hours, then examine your face in a mirror, using good, natural light. Now answer the questions on the chart (page 15).
4. Allow your face to remain makeup-free for the rest of the day.
5. Around five or six P.M., take another close look at your face in good light and answer the questions again. Notice if anything has changed.
6. Cleanse your face the way you did in the morning, rinse, and pat dry.
7. **Don't put anything on your face before going to bed.**
8. Immediately upon awakening in the morning, examine your face closely in good, natural light. Answer the questions a third time.

You have **oily skin** if:

- you answered *yes* consistently to questions 1 and 2 and checked all four boxes.
- you answered *no* to questions 3, 4, and 5.

First examination—two hours after washing

	YES	NO		NOSE	FORE-HEAD	CHIN	CHEEKS
	(check one)			(check as many as apply)			
1. Can you *see* any oil?	☐	☐	*Where?*	☐	☐	☐	☐
2. Can you *feel* any oil?	☐	☐	*Where?*	☐	☐	☐	☐
3. Can you *see* any dryness?	☐	☐	*Where?*	☐	☐	☐	☐
4. Can you *feel* any dryness?	☐	☐	*Where?*	☐	☐	☐	☐
5. Does the skin feel tight and look chalky?	☐	☐					
6. Does the skin feel tight and look smooth?	☐	☐					

Second examination—early evening

	YES	NO		NOSE	FORE-HEAD	CHIN	CHEEKS
	(check one)			(check as many as apply)			
1. Can you *see* any oil?	☐	☐	*Where?*	☐	☐	☐	☐
2. Can you *feel* any oil?	☐	☐	*Where?*	☐	☐	☐	☐
3. Can you *see* any dryness?	☐	☐	*Where?*	☐	☐	☐	☐
4. Can you *feel* any dryness?	☐	☐	*Where?*	☐	☐	☐	☐
5. Does the skin feel tight and look chalky?	☐	☐					
6. Does the skin feel tight and look smooth?	☐	☐					

Third examination—the next morning

	YES	NO		NOSE	FORE-HEAD	CHIN	CHEEKS
	(check one)			(check as many as apply)			
1. Can you *see* any oil?	☐	☐	*Where?*	☐	☐	☐	☐
2. Can you *feel* any oil?	☐	☐	*Where?*	☐	☐	☐	☐
3. Can you *see* any dryness?	☐	☐	*Where?*	☐	☐	☐	☐
4. Can you *feel* any dryness?	☐	☐	*Where?*	☐	☐	☐	☐
5. Does the skin feel tight and look chalky?	☐	☐					
6. Does the skin feel tight and look smooth?	☐	☐					

You have **dry skin** if:

- you answered *yes* to questions 3 and 4 and checked all four boxes.
- you answered *yes* to question 5.
- you answered *no* to questions 1, 2, and 6.

You have **combination skin** *to the oily side* if:

- you consistently answered *yes* to question 1 and checked two or three out of four boxes.
- you consistently answered *yes* to question 2, and checked two or three out of four boxes.
- You answered *no* to questions 3, 4, and 5.

You have **combination skin** *to the dry side* if:

- you consistently answered *yes* to questions 3 and 4 and checked two out of four boxes.
- you answered *yes* to question 5 one or more times.

You have **true combination skin** if:

- you answered *yes* to questions 1 and 2 in the evening and/or upon awakening, and the boxes you checked changed.
- you answered *yes* to questions 3, 4, and 6 one or two times.
- you answered *no* to question 5.

You have **normal (or balanced) skin** if:

- you answered *yes* to questions 1 and/or 2 upon awakening and checked one or two boxes.
- you answered *yes* consistently to question 6.
- you answered *no* to questions 3, 4, and 5.

Basic Rules
for Skin Types

If you have **oily skin**:

1. Stay away from rich, oil-based soaps which contain coconut oil or cocoa butter.

2. **Never** use oil-based "milky" cleansers or any cleanser that is used without water.

3. Never use a moisturizer. Instead, use pure aloe vera gel as both toner and moisturizer.

4. Use an astringent during the day as well as part of your twice-a-day skin care routine.

5. Use a water-based foundation to help absorb oil during the day.

6. Use a "scrub" once or twice a week only. Frequent scrubbing activates the already overly active oil glands.

7. Don't use a loofa, Buff Puff, or wash cloth; these also activate oil glands.

8. Cut down on oil- or fat-rich foods such as cheeses, dairy products, fried foods, nuts, and so on.

9. **Drink eight glasses of water a day.** (Some of those can be herbal teas) to help flush out toxins and excess oils.

10. **Keep your hands off your face!** (Bacteria is transmitted and thrives in oil.)

11. **Choose a hair style that keeps hair off the face.**

12. Don't use baby oil or oil-based cleansers to remove eye makeup (unless they are water-soluble oils).

13. If skin becomes excessively oily while you sleep, apply a *very thin* layer of calamine lotion before going to bed.

If you have **dry skin:**

1. Use a mild, nondrying soap or cleanser.

2. Make sure your diet contains a reasonable amount of fats and oils.

3. Discontinue use of dehydrating substances such as caffeine, cigarettes, excessive alcohol, and drugs.

4. Drink eight glasses of water daily.

5. Don't use dry saunas.

6. Use a humidifier in your bedroom.

7. Use pure aloe vera gel as a toner.

8. Use a natural oil-based moisturizer.

9. Exercise regularly. (This brings oxygen to the skin and helps it to maintain its natural moisture. Dry skin is thought of as being "sluggish.")

10. **Stay out of the sun.** If you must be out in strong sunlight, use a sunblock with an SPF of 15 or more.

11. Do a two-month vitamin therapy program:

- Vitamin A   25,000 units 2 x daily with meals
- Vitamin E   800 units 1 x daily with meals
- Zinc   30 mgs. 1 x daily with meals
- B Complex   50 mgs. 2 x daily with meals

After one month, cut down to 25,000 units of A once daily and keep other dosages the same. After two months, discontinue the zinc and the A and cut down to 400 units of E. You can continue the B complex. Notice any changes in your skin during the two months of therapy as well as when you stop. If signs of dryness begin to reappear, repeat the two-month program again.

12. Don't use products containing mineral oil.

13. Try to avoid swings in weight and drastic diets.

14. Avoid diuretic pills and use Select's KB11 Herb Tea instead to combat bloat. Most health food stores stock this tea. Any herbal tea will have a mild diuretic effect, but the KB11 is stronger than any others.

15. Don't use astringents or toners with astringent qualities.

If you have **combination skin:**

1. Be sure to use products designed for oily skin on oily areas **only,** and do the same with products for normal or dry areas.

2. Be aware, on a daily basis, of subtle changes in the degrees of oiliness and dryness. Most combination skin fluctuates. Your regime won't be the same all the time.

3. Notice how changes in diet may affect the balance of your skin.

4. Use a cleanser that is gentle enough for the dry-normal areas, but clears the oil from the oily areas.

If you have **normal skin:**

1. Use a mild soap or cleanser designed for normal skin.

2. Don't use astringents.

3. Use aloe vera gel as a toner-moisturizer to protect and maintain balance.

4. Use a natural oil-based moisturizer **only when necessary,** such as in extreme weather conditions or climate changes.

5. **Keep up the good work—you're doing something right!**

If you have **aging skin:**

1. Follow the basic rules for your skin type.

2. Meet with a nutritionist who can recommend a vitamin supplementation program designed to combat the aging process. The book *Life Extension* by Durk Pearson and Sandy Shaw (Warner Books, 1982) has a wealth of information on this and many other topics.

3. Daily aerobic exercise for twenty minutes or more will help to increase circulation and bring oxygen to the blood and skin.

4. Add vitamin E to moisturizer and facial masks by breaking open a capsule of 400 I.U.'s or more and squeezing the contents into the product.

5. Monthly professional facials will insure removal of dead skin cells which emphasize tiny lines and give the skin a dull appearance.

6. Drink six to eight glasses of water daily. This helps to "plump up" or "hydrate" tired, dehydrated skin.

7. Use a sun block with an SPF of 15 or more and avoid the sun as much as possible.

8. Eliminate dehydrating substances such as caffeine and cigarettes from your diet, and limit the amount of alcohol you drink.

If your skin is prone to **breakouts** or **acne:**

1. Be as gentle as possible with your skin. Stay away from harsh scrubs, loofas, Buff Puffs, and wash cloths. These activate the oil glands and aggravate existing pimples.

2. Visit a dermatologist to see if Acutane, a revolutionary treatment for acne, would be appropriate for you. This treatment clears acne permanently.

3. Use an astringent several times during the day (on oily areas and blemishes) as well as during your twice-daily skin care routine.

4. Use products with as few chemicals and preservatives as possible.

5. Keep hands off the face.

6. **Eliminate iodine** from the diet. This has been found to be the major cause of acne. Foods high in iodine are: red meat (this is not naturally high in iodine, however, cattle are fed iodized salt licks); any seafood or saltwater fish; iodized salt; kelp (this can be in vitamins and seasoned salts); dairy products (dairy machinery is cleaned with an iodine solution to sanitize it).

7. Eliminate all forms of caffeine from the diet.

8. Eliminate refined sugars from the diet.

9. Eliminate as many chemicals as possible from the diet. This means artificial coloring, flavoring, preservatives, and so on.

10. Eat as much fresh, raw, or simply cooked food as possible, such as vegetables, fruits, whole grains, poultry, and so on.

11. Don't attempt do-it-yourself surgery on blemishes; you could drive the infection deeper and cause scarring. See a dermatologist or reliable facialist who can open pimples properly.

12. Use calamine lotion with phenol, applied in two layers, on blemishes.

13. Use aloe vera gel over your astringent and under makeup base. This protects and balances the skin.

14. Refer to the face chart on page 47 to see why you may be breaking out in certain areas.

15. Use astringent and calamine lotion on blemishes in any other areas such as shoulders, back, or chest.

Part Two

TAKING CARE OF YOUR SKIN

Seven Basic Steps
for Cleansing

The actual process of washing the face, or cleansing, may be the most important step toward beautiful, healthy skin. To understand why, let me explain how the skin works.

The outer layer that we can see and touch is made up of dry, dead cells. The younger, living cells which make up several layers beneath the skin's surface are continually maturing as they move up toward the surface of the skin. By the time they reach the outer layer they have died and will eventually fall off. Ideally, the faster we can keep this process going, and the more efficiently we can rid the skin of the old cells, the younger and healthier the skin will appear.

So, one of the purposes of daily cleansing is to help remove the outer layer of dried cells.

An important thing to know is that these outer cells are arranged in a downward direction, like fish scales. This is why using an upward, circular massaging motion is recommended for cleansing—this gets up and under the cells for easy removal.

For the same reason, masks, toners, and makeup base should always be applied in a downward direction to smooth out the cells and create a smooth finish.

The other purpose of daily cleansing is to rid the skin of surface dirt and oil that can clog pores.

The seven basic steps should be followed two to three times a day, no matter what skin type you are. Wash for the first time in the morning. The second cleansing should take place at the end of the day, which might be at four P.M. for some and nine P.M. for others. The object of this washing is to "wash the day off your face," as my mother used to say. You'll be getting rid of day-old makeup as well as oils, dirt, and pollutants. If you apply fresh makeup to go out for the evening, be sure to cleanse before going to bed. If you do something active during the day like running, aerobics, or the like be sure to cleanse afterward also. It's great to perspire but remember that perspiration carries toxins out of the body, and it's not a good idea to let them remain on the skin. It's also important to rehydrate the skin after working out.

At first, the Seven Steps may look like a lot to do but the actual time they take is only three minutes.

Step One: Wash

Use a cleanser or soap appropriate for your skin type. The wrong cleanser can cause problems such as drying skin out or making it more oily. Use the hands in a circular motion, emphasizing the upward movement. This helps to remove the dead, outer layer of cells.

Relax the face. Making faces makes lines. Relaxing the face makes this a pleasant experience. Don't pull the skin. This destroys the skin's elasticity.

Massage with cleanser for a full minute and a half. It takes this long to soften the skin and move the pores around enough to loosen dirt and dissolve oil. This is a great preventive measure against whiteheads and blackheads.

Note: Women with dry skin, or combination skin to the dry side, should apply 1 tablespoon of the following mixture to the face before applying soap. The soap and oil should then be massaged together: 1 oz. almond oil, 1 oz. avocado oil, 1 oz. sunflower oil.

Step Two: Rinse

Use *comfortably* hot, running water. Water that is too hot can break capillaries and dehydrate the skin. If water is too cool most cleansers and soaps won't work effectively. Splash 20 to 30 times. It takes 20 to 30 splashes to remove most cleansers and soaps. Also, the skin needs water from external as well as internal sources to be plump and fresh-looking.

Step Three: Pat Dry

Use a clean, soft towel. Towels should be free of dirt or bacteria, and soft so as not to scratch the skin. Don't rub or pull the skin. Rubbing and pulling stretches the skin, causing it to lose elasticity.

Step Four: Apply Astringent

The only people who need astringents are those with oily skin. People with combination skin should use astringents *on oily areas only.* If an astringent is used on a normal or dry area it will dehydrate the skin and cause redness and dryness. If you need to use an astringent, apply using a cotton ball or pad. Astringent is to be left on after application.

Step Five: Apply Toner

Toners do several things: they bring the pH of the skin down and set up the acid mantle; they tighten or "tone" the skin, which creates a smooth finish by helping to close down the pores; and they act as a protective base for applying makeup. The toner that I recommend *for all skin types* is natural aloe vera gel. It fulfills all of the requirements of a toner and more. By attracting oxygen it helps the skin to hold moisture. It tightens the skin so much that it feels like a "mini-facelift," but will absolutely *not* dry out the skin.

To apply, pour two to three tablespoons of gel into the palm of your hand. Spread it over both palms and apply to the entire face and neck. The face should be soaking wet. Toner is to be left on after application.

Step Six: Apply Moisturizer (If Necessary)

The only people who should use moisturizer are those with truly dry skin. People with combination skin to the dry side may use moisturizer on dry areas only.

Step Seven: Apply Eye Oil

Everyone needs eye oil to protect and nourish the extremely delicate tissue around the eyes. This is the thinnest skin on the entire body, and there are no oil glands in the eye area. This means no natural lubrication in an area used constantly for a multitude of expressions such as blinking, laughing, squinting, and crying.

There are, unfortunately, very few good eye oils on the market. Most are petrolatum (Vaseline) or mineral oil-based, making them too heavy to be used under makeup as well as ultimately dehydrating. Imagine applying eye makeup over Vaseline. These oils and creams should also never be used before bedtime because, combined with the body's slight rise in temperature at night, they cause swelling.

Product Recommendations

Before you read the product description and recommendation list, I want to restate which products are necessary for each skin type.

If you have **dry skin** you need:

- Natural oil mixture for washing
- Nondrying low-pH cleanser or soap
- Aloe vera gel toner
- Oil-based moisture oil or moisturizer
- Eye oil
- Very mild and gentle deep pore cleanser (not to exceed twice weekly).

If you have **oily skin** you need:

- Soap or cleanser for oily skin
- Astringent
- Aloe vera gel toner
- Eye oil (if any dryness in eye area)
- Deep pore cleanser (not to exceed twice weekly)
- Calamine lotion with phenol for breakouts

If you have **combination skin to the dry side** you need:

- Natural oil mixture for washing
- Nondrying low-pH cleanser or soap
- Astringent (on oily areas only)
- Aloe vera gel toner (all over)
- Oil-based moisture oil or moisturizer (dry areas only)
- Eye oil
- Deep pore cleanser (not to exceed twice weekly)

If you have **combination skin to the oily side** you need:

- Soap or cleanser for combination to oily skin
- Astringent (on oily areas only)
- Aloe vera gel toner (all over)
- Eye oil (if any dryness in eye area)
- Calamine lotion with phenol for breakouts
- Deep pore cleanser (not to exceed twice weekly)

If you have **normal skin** you need:

- Mild soap or cleanser for normal skin
- Aloe vera gel toner
- Eye oil
- Deep pore cleanser (not to exceed twice weekly)

Cleansers

Remember, the purpose of a cleanser is twofold, it should help to remove the outer layer of dead, dry cells, as well as to cleanse the skin. If dirt, oils, and toxins aren't removed, they cause blackheads, whiteheads and blemishes.

There are three basic types of cleansers: soaps, "milky cleansers," and cleansing gels.

Soaps have a variety of bases such as animal fat, seaweed, vegetable or other oil, clay, oatmeal, or synthetic detergent. I recommend "natural" soaps that have a low pH because they won't dry out the skin. "Soapless soaps" are detergent-free and free of animal fats as well. They are excellent for all skin types, as well as for people who are allergic to soap, or who have sensitive skin.

The following key denotes which skin type the product is recommended for:

D = dry
O = oily
CD = combination to the dry side
CO = combination to the oily side
N = normal
A = acne
T = all skin types

The key denotes where products can be purchased:

H = health food store
P = pharmacy
DS = department store

Recommendations:

• Cooper Laboratory's Aveenobar	T	P
• Estée Lauder's Basic Cleansing Bar	O,CO,N	DS
• Ortho Pharmaceutical's Purpose	T	P
• Terme di Montecatini Clarifying Cleansing Cream (soap)	T	DS
• Pierre Cattier's Nature de France	T	H
• Steifel Laboratory's Oilatum	D,CD,N	P
• Perscriptives Cleansing Lather Bar (soapless)	T	DS
• Westwood Pharmaceutical's Lowila	T	P

Milky cleansers are oil-based emulsions which are massaged into the skin and tissued off. I don't recommend most commercial versions of this type of cleanser because they are mineral oil-based. The oil remains on the skin and can cause dehydration, since mineral oil inhibits the skin's ability to retain moisture. It also acts as a magnet for dirt because it remains on the surface of the skin. In addition, it "seals" the skin, trapping toxins rather than allowing them to be released, and prevents oxygen from entering.

Recommendations:

• Aubrey Organic's Natural Organic Facial Cleanser	D	H
• Clientele Moisture Concentrate (use with Clientele soap)	T	DS
• Elizabeth Arden's Gentle Cleansing Emulsion	D	H
• Germaine Monteil's Active Cleansing Concentrate	O	DS
• Naturade's Deep Cleansing Lotion	D,CD	H
• Perscriptive Cleansing Lather	N	DS
• Rachael Perry's Citrus Cleanser and Face Wash	D	H

Cleansing gels are thick, synthetic-based cleansers which can be good for people who are allergic to soap, provided they have a low pH. They are also handy for travel since they come in tubes or plastic squeeze bottles.

Recommendations:

• Estée Lauder's Thorough Cleansing Gel	N,O,CO	DS
• Germaine Monteil's Gentle Acting Gel Cleanser	N,O,CO	DS
• Germaine Monteil's Clarity Super Cleanser	O,CO,A	DS
• Neolife's Clarifying Cleanser*	O,CO,A	DS

*This is sold through private distributors. Check your local phone book under "Neolife," for the one nearest you.

Deep Pore Cleansers

Deep pore cleansers are designed to slough off even more dead cells than a cleanser. These products have a grainy texture and are also called *sloughing creams, exfoliating creams,* and *facial scrubs.*

Note: If you have acne I recommend using a medicated scrub recommended by your dermatologist, not more than twice a week.

Recommendations:

- Aubrey Organic's Jojoba Meal and Oatmeal
  Facial Scrub and Mask   T H
- Aubrey Organic's Meal N'Herbs   T H
- Clinique's Exfoliating Cream   T DS
- Ralph Lauren's Almond Scrub   T DS
- Helena Rubenstein's Face Buffing Cream   T DS
- Rachael Perry's Sea Kelp Herbal Facial Scrub   T H

An excellent deep pore cleanser can be homemade by mixing together, in a small bowl, the following ingredients: 1 tsp. cornmeal; 1 tsp. crushed oats; 1 tsp. honey; and 1 tsp. plain yogurt.

Astringents

The purpose of an astringent is to help absorb excess oil which acts as a breeding ground for bacteria. A good astringent will contain one or more forms of alcohol, witch hazel, alum, citrus, or other antiseptics. Astringents usually sting or tingle on the skin and should be used *on oily areas only.* If used on a dry or normal skin area, an astringent will cause redness, followed by dryness that can peel and flake. If an astringent causes these symptoms *on an oily area* it is too strong and should not be used.

Clinique's Clarifying Lotions #2 and #3 or any others that contain acetone, the main ingredient in fingernail polish remover, should be avoided. This chemical is too harsh to use on the skin.

The only people who need to use astringents are those with oily skin, or people with combination skin, who would use it *on oily areas only.*

Recommendations:

• Aubrey Organic's Herbal Facial Astringent	O,CO	H
• Aubrey Organic's Amino Derm Gel	O,A	H
• Germaine Monteil's Super Tone Skin Conditioner	O,CO	DS
• Germaine Monteil's Clarity Oil Absorbant	O,CO	DS
• Nature's Gate Facial Toner	O,CO,A	H
• Rachael Perry's Lemon Mist Astringent	O,CO,A	H

A good astringent can be homemade by mixing together, in a glass jar, the following ingredients: 3 ozs. witch hazel; 3 ozs. aloe vera gel or juice; and 1 tsp. alum. This mixture should be kept in the refrigerator. For convenience, a small bottle may be kept in the bathroom and refilled once a week.

Toners

The purpose of a toner, as the name implies, is to "tone" the skin. This means helping to close down the pores after they've been opened by cleansing. When the pores are closed, a smooth, tight surface is created. Ideally, a toner should also adjust the pH of the skin, so that the protective acid mantle is replaced.

Unfortunately, cosmetic companies don't make proper distinctions between toners and astringents, so it's up to you to read labels. If a "toner" contains alcohol, witch hazel, or other antiseptics, it is not a true toner, but an astringent. Natural toners usually contain some form of citrus, aloe vera, or soothing herbs such as hamamelis, camomile, cucumber, cornflower extract, horse chestnut, and so on.

All skin types need a toner. My favorite one, for all skin types including acne or problem skin, is pure aloe vera gel. This is an extract of the aloe vera plant. It has very effective healing/soothing qualities and fulfills all the requirements of a toner and more. It is a natural oxygenator. This means that it helps your skin to hold oxygen, and skin that holds oxygen also holds its own natural moisture. So aloe vera acts as a toner and moisturizer.

Most health food stores offer several brands of aloe vera gel, but to be sure you're getting the real thing, read the label. It should contain between 95 and 99 percent aloe vera. Don't confuse this pure product with others called "aloe vera toner, aloe vera moisturizer," and so on. These others are usually water- or oil-based products bearing no resemblance to real aloe vera gel.

A quality aloe vera gel usually contains one or more of the following ingredients: Irish moss (thickener), sorbic acid (natural preservative), citric acid (natural preservative), ascorbic acid (Vitamin C used as a natural preservative).

Because natural aloe vera gel is not chemically preserved it should be refrigerated after opening. For convenience, pour some into a small bottle to keep in the bathroom and refill it once a week. It's also a good idea to pour the gel into your hand to avoid contact with the container. This way you won't transfer bacteria from hands to bottle.

Recommendations:

- Dr. Donsbach's Aloe Vera Gel   T   H
- Radiance Aloe Vera Gel   T   H
- Real Aloe Vera Gel (this is the brand name)   T   H
- RichLife Aloe Vera Gel   T   H

Moisturizer

The purpose of a moisturizer is to help the skin hold its natural moisture. Basically, we can divide moisturizers into three main categories as far as composition: mineral oil-based, natural oil-based, and water-based.

The only moisturizers I recommend are natural oil-based. Unfortunately these are not very common. Most commercial cosmetic companies use either mineral oil or purified water as bases. The problem with these bases is this: Mineral oil is a by-product of the petroleum industry. It is a thinned-out version of Vaseline. Baby oil is simply mineral oil with fragrance. As I mentioned earlier, when mineral oil is applied to the skin, it seals it.

Common symptoms of mineral oil use are blackheads, whiteheads, and little bumps, just under the surface of the skin. Mineral oil also acts as a magnet for dirt because it remains on the surface of the skin (and builds up), rather than being absorbed. The final result is usually problem skin as well as dehydration.

Some other common ingredients found in these commercial, mineral oil-based moisturizers are just as bad as mineral oil—if not more dangerous. *The most common ones to avoid are:*

- Beeswax—has the same effect as mineral oil
- Carbomer 934 (thickener)—can cause eye irritation
- Isopropyl Myristate (emollient)—causes irritation and clogs pores
- Lanolin (emollient)—a fatty substance derived from the wool of sheep and an allergen for some people.
- Petrolatum (Vaseline)

The point is this: not only do most commercial moisturizers contain questionable if not dangerous ingredients, they don't fulfill the promises they make. And there is little or no basis for the enormous prices of these creams, aside from packaging and advertising costs.

Water-based or "oil-free" moisturizers are composed of purified water plus chemicals. The only difference between these and mineral oil-based creams is the omission of mineral oil.

Natural oil-based moisturizers are usually made with oils such as safflower, almond, jojoba, avocado, and so on. These are light enough to be partially or wholly absorbed by the skin and to act as the skin's natural oils, that is, help the skin to hold moisture. Both of the recommended products may be worn under makeup.

Recommendations for Daytime Moisturizers:

- Desert Essence Moisture Cream   D,CD   H
- Nature's Gate Moisture Cream   D,CD   H

Examples of good natural oil moisturizers designed to be used at night are ones made by Clarins. They contain hazelnut, patchouli, rosewood, and vegetal (wheat germ) oils. There are no chemicals. Some contain fragrance, but I believe this is natural.

Recommendations for Nighttime Moisturizers:

- Clarins Huile Orchidee Bleue   D,CD   DS
- Clarins Huile Santal   D,CD   DS

Eye Oil

The purpose of an eye oil is to protect and lubricate the delicate skin around the eyes. This skin is the thinnest on the entire body. There are also no oil glands around the eyes to provide much needed lubrication. Ideally, an eye oil should be water soluble and/or quickly absorbed because any residue left on the skin will cause eye makeup to smudge and run. Eye oil should be used twice a day, as part of your cleansing routine.

Unfortunately, very few cosmetic companies make good eye oils, especially the major cosmetic companies. La Prairie, for example, sells for $55 for .6 ozs. It contains two of the cheapest and worst ingredients: mineral oil and petrolatum.

The complete list of ingredients reads: water, mineral oil, polyglycolic ester (unable to identify), petrolatum (Vaseline), acetylated lanolin (a more acceptable form of lanolin), propylene glycol (solvent, conditioner, humectant) placenta cells (no proven effect on the skin), carbomer 934 (thickener, can cause eye irritation), trilaneth 45-phosphate (complex lanolin derivative, okay), propyl and methyl parabens (preservatives, okay), imidazolidinyl urea (preservative, okay), triethanolamine (questionable), collagen (does nothing when applied topically), hypericum extract (soothing herb), mallow extract (soothing herb), St. John's Wort flower extract (soothing herb). Notice that the most beneficial and expensive ingredients are listed last, indicating very small amounts.

Another important fact to know about eye oils is that if you use them at night they will cause swelling. Any oil or oil-based creams which are not water-soluble, applied to the eyes at night, will cause swelling because of the body's slight rise in temperature.

Recommendations:

- Earth Science Eye Oil and Remover (not water-soluble)   T H
- Zia for Eyes Eye Oil and Makeup Remover (Mail order. $12 plus $1 postage to P.O. Box 143, Mill Valley, California 94941) Water soluble.

Sloughing or Exfoliating Creams and Scrubs

The purpose of sloughing creams, exfoliating creams, and scrubs is to remove the skin's outer layer of dry, dead cells. Proper cleansing will help to remove these cells on a daily basis, but once- or twice-weekly use of one of these creams will get the job done more thoroughly. These creams and scrubs also help to lessen and/or prevent superficial lines.

There are several things you should know about sloughing and exfoliating creams and scrubs.

1. Use them gently with no pressure. Let the grains do the work. Rubbing hard can damage the living cells which lie beneath the skin's surface.

2. Massage with an upward circular motion, as in cleansing, for one to two minutes.

3. Excessive use (more than twice a week) can be too harsh on the skin and, for oily skin, will activate the oil glands too much, causing them to produce even more oil.

4. They should not be used on acne or pimples.

5. If you are prone to broken capillaries be sure to use the finest, most gentle product.

6. Avoid products containing sharp, hard particles because these can actually cause tiny cuts on the skin. The ideal texture should feel like salt if you mixed it with a creamy substance.

7. If the cream you're using has a mineral oil, beeswax, or petrolatum base, use it before cleansing so that it may be washed off completely.

Masks

Masks have several functions: they can tighten the skin, making pores appear to be smaller; absorb excess oil and help to draw out blackheads and clogged pores; calm down aggravated or acned skin; and they may also nourish and feed the skin. All masks made by commercial cosmetic companies are nothing more than chemical compounds. I do not recommend any of them.

Natural cosmetic companies make some good masks, but regardless of what they are called, most seem to have the same function: to absorb excess oil and draw out toxins. This means that the main ingredient is some form, or several forms, of clay. Kaolin, bentonite, and montmorillonite are the most common clays used in masks. Because clay absorbs two hundred times its weight in water, it is very dehydrating.

If you have oily or acned skin clay masks are fine. If you have combination or normal skin I suggest you use these masks very sparingly, not more than once a month, for seven or eight minutes.

If you have dry skin, avoid masks which contain clay.

Recommended clay-based masks:

- Desert Essence Jojoba Facial Mask   O,CO,N   H
- Fuller's Earth   O,CO,N   P
- Kiehl's Rare Earth Facial Mask   O,CO,N   H
- Nature's Gate Facial Mask   T   H
- Pierre Cattier's Nature de France French
  Clay Mask   O,CO   H
- Terme di Montecatini Fango   T   DS

The only masks which truly feed and nourish the skin are those you make yourself. These are combinations of fresh foods and vitamins that you mix up by hand or in a blender.

In the spring and summer beauty and health magazines always publish articles on homemade masks which include recipes. Natural cosmetic books also give good recipes for masks.

Here are a couple of my recipes which are good for all skin types. These masks are applied to the entire face and neck, with the exception of the eye area, and may be left on for 15 to 20 minutes. More recipes can be found in my book *Being Beautiful,* Whatever Publishing, 1983.

Avocado Mask: In a blender place: ½ ripe avocado, ⅛ cup plain yogurt, 2″ slice of cucumber (without skin); blend until smooth, then apply.

Buttermilk Mask: Let a 4–6 oz. glass of buttermilk stand, unrefrigerated, overnight. In the morning, skim the thick curds off the top and apply to face. This doesn't smell too great, but is very soothing and nourishing.

Recommendations:
See **Recommendations** for deep pore cleansers, on p. 32.

Exfoliating Masks

These are applied to the face, left on for approximately five minutes, then rubbed off. They can be irritating to some skin and should never be used by people with sensitive skin or acne. Also, because of the rubbing needed to remove them, they can have the same effect as shaving on superficial facial hairs.

Most exfoliating masks have a wax or paraffin base and should be washed from the skin with cleanser after use.

I don't recommend these masks for the reasons I've given above and because I feel that good grainy scrubs are more effective and less apt to be damaging.

"Miracle Treatments"

There are dozens of creams, lotions, oils, and ampules which fall into this category. Every cosmetic line offers something which promises to correct our worst flaws and fulfill our dreams of perfection. Unfortunately, if you read the labels on these products you'll usually find them to be strikingly similar to other products in the line.

Very often "miracle treatments" will contain the latest "revolutionary ingredient." I'm sure you'll remember some of these: bee pollen, turtle oil, hormones, placenta, collagen, and elastin. The list goes on to include two of the newest discoveries: "equine serum" and "bovine extract," courtesy of our friends the horse and the cow. Every few months multimillion-dollar ad campaigns bombard us with cleverly-worded promises and supposed facts. But personally, I've never been able to find written proof as a result of independent testing of any of these claims. I've also never met a woman who used one of these treatments and got the results as promised on the package.

Prices of these products range from about $8 to $150. These "miracle treatments" and any other so-called anti-aging or perpetual youth creams represent the epitome of hype, and women of all ages and all income brackets are taken in by them. What's important to understand is that, to date, no one has found a way to erase the signs of aging by any means other than plastic surgery, silicone or collagen injections, and sometimes acupressure or acupuncture "facelifting." What you put in your body in the way of vitamins and wholesome foods will do a thousand times more for anti-aging than anything you put on it.

Just for fun, let's take a look at the ingredients in two extremely expensive "miracle" products made by one of the most well-known cosmetic companies in the world.

"Wrinkle Cream": Acetylated lanolin (emollient, a more acceptable form than pure lanolin); water; beeswax (seals skin, clogs pores, builds up with use); montmorillonite (natural clay, absorbs 200 times its weight in water, making it incredibly dehydrating); collagen (useless when applied topically); propylene glycol (solvent and conditioner; humectant); sodium borate (a detergent builder, emulsifier, and preservative); cholesterol (a sterol, used as an emulsifier); placenta cells (useless); and methyl paraben and ethyl paraben (preservatives and possible sensitizers).

Now let's compare the "Wrinkle Cream" with the "Cellular Day Cream."

"Cellular Day Cream": water (same); acetylated lanolin (same); ceteareth 12 (an emulsion stabilizer and/or emulsifier); propylene glycol (same); parafitin (beeswax . . . how clever. same); triethanolamine (TEA, alkalyzing agent, questionable); carbomer 934 (a thickener; can cause eye irritation); trilaneth-4 phosphate (complex lanolin derivative); placenta cells (same);

methyl paraben (same); ethyl paraben (same); propyl paraben (same); Dermodors (an unknown substance, called a "secret ingredient," but judging from its placement, a minute quantity anyway).

The "wrinkle cream,"—which sells for $50 per 1 oz.—has 12 ingredients, eight of which are found in the "Cellular Day Cream," which sells for $65 an oz. Two are another form of lanolin, one is a thickener and possible irritant, one is an alkalyzing agent and known carcinogen, and one is an unknown substance.

So, basically what we have here are two essentially identical creams distinguished only by two questionable ingredients in one—montmorillonite and collagen—and two possibly dangerous ingredients in the other—TEA and carbomer 934.

Post Script

I'd like to add one final piece of information which is equally as important as everything I've discussed thus far.

Our friend, the sun—which many of us grew up worshipping—isn't such a great friend after all. The incidence of skin cancer among Americans has tripled in the past few years and continues to escalate. If that isn't frightening enough, consider this: The sun will age skin faster than anything else. You won't see the damage for five or ten years, but once it's done, it's irreversible. No miracle creams will correct this damage; nothing short of surgery or collagen injections will.

If you love outdoor sports, as I do, please take the precaution to use a sun block with an SPF (sun protection factor) of at least 15. There are dozens on the market to choose from. Find one that you like and use it.

Part Three

SKIN PROBLEM SOLVING

Breakouts:
Their Variety
and Treatment

Whiteheads

Whiteheads are usually small to medium in size (the size of the head of a pin or a bit larger), with a soft, white head above the surface of the skin. One method of treatment is the "do-it-yourself facial." Steam the face for five to eight minutes. Then use a grainy cleanser or scrub cream and gently massage, using the hands in a circular motion for a minute or two. Rinse well and apply a pure clay mask—like Pierre Cattier's French Rose Clay Mask—to draw out any remaining toxins. Leave the mask on for 10 to 15 minutes, rinse well, and apply aloe vera gel. If any whiteheads still remain, apply either calamine lotion with phenol or one of the "emergency masks" to the heads only and leave on overnight. The following emergency masks are recommended:

* Clinique's Beauty Non-Drying Emergency Mask   DS
* Germaine Monteil's Medicated Treatment with
  Colodial Sulphur   DS
* Payot's Pate Grisse   DS

Blackheads

Blackheads are individual pores which become clogged and appear grey or black beneath the surface of the skin. The most effective way to remove blackheads is to get a professional, deep-cleansing facial. The do-it-yourself facial can help if the blackheads are not too deep. Regular cleansing and weekly at-home facials, along with frequent daily use of a mild astringent, will help prevent blackheads. Wearing a water-base foundation will protect the skin from pollutants and dirt and help to absorb excess oil during the day. (See "Bases"—pp. 52–55—for brand names.)

Calcium Deposits (or uric acid deposits)

These deposits look like whiteheads but they have a hard head rather than a soft one. You *cannot* remove these yourself. They have to be surgically removed by a dermatologist. The doctor can order a lab analysis to determine the composition of the deposit. If it is calcium, cut down on calcium-rich foods such as dairy products. If it is a uric acid deposit, cut down on red meats.

Skin Bumps

Sometimes small bumps which don't come to a head appear beneath the surface of the skin. These bumps can usually be attributed to an allergic reaction to a cosmetic. Simplify your skin-care routine, eliminating moisturizer and replacing it with pure aloe vera gel. Flushing the body with eight glasses of water a day will also help to clear up skin bumps.

Breakouts:
Their Cause
and Cure

The illustration on p. 47 shows areas of breakouts on the face and what the possible cause might be. The drawing enumerates six areas on the face and the major organs that they correspond to, according to traditional Chinese acupuncture diagnoses. If you have persistent breakouts (in some instances, specific kinds of breakouts) in one area you may want to consult an acupuncturist to balance the weak organ.

Number on Face	Possible Cause of Breakout	Corresponding Organ
1	Poor diet	Stomach
2	Poor elimination of toxins	Large intestine
3 (blackheads)	Insufficient digestive enzymes	Thyroid, Pituitary, Adrenal
4 (blackheads)	Poor metabolism	Small intestine
5 (pimples)	Poor diet; high fat content	Gall bladder
6	Stress	Brain

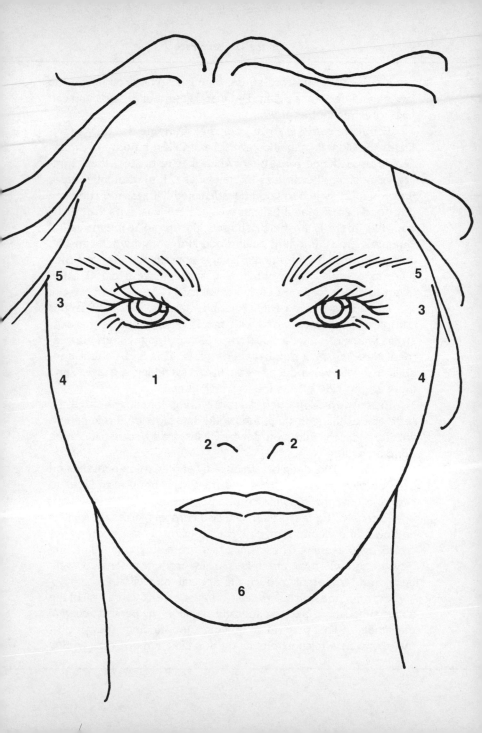

If you break out from **stress,** blemishes will occur along the jawline and/or onto the chin. There are a number of steps you can take to eliminate the problem.

Eliminate caffeine from your diet. Caffeine not only dehydrates the skin, it magnifies even the smallest amount of stress. People use caffeine most often when they're rushed, tired, hungry, or pushing themselves to stay awake. If it's the coffee taste that you love, switch to good decaffeinated coffees. You can even buy good decaffeinated teas, as well as herb teas. If it's the "rush" you like, there is an herb, shaped like a vanilla bean, called Guaranna. You'll find it in health food stores in powder, capsule, and tea forms. If your energy level is consistently low you may want to consult with a nutritionist, and/or have a blood count taken to check for iron deficiency anemia.

Make sure you're getting enough vitamins. Take a 50 mg. B complex three times a day with meals. This is one of the anti-stress vitamins. Take a *1000 mg.* calcium/magnesium supplement *three times a day* between meals. This is a natural tranquilizer. It will even induce sleep if five to six tablets are taken, and there are no side effects the morning after.

Relax yourself through deep breathing. Inhaling through the nose and exhaling through the mouth in a slow rhythmic pattern will immediately calm you down. This is great because it can be done anywhere.

Meditate. Like deep breathing, a five or ten minute meditation can completely relieve stress and may even bring insights as to why and how the situation came about in the first place.

Exercise. The reason that exercise combats stress (as well as tiredness and depression) is because of the beta endorfins secreted by the brain. These enzymes are also produced during orgasm and when we are in love. They produce a sense of well-being and temporarily reduce the appetite as well.

Examine the reasons for stress in your life. If you try all of the above suggestions and the stressful situation still persists, *change the situation!* That may mean quitting a job, finding a new roommate, or a new relationship. If you don't like what stress is doing to your face, imagine what your insides look like. This is the stuff that ulcers are made of.

If you break out from *poor elimination,* blackheads, whiteheads, or pimples will show up where the nostrils meet the cheek. There are several ways to respond to this problem as well.

Drink eight glasses of water a day. This flushes out toxins. Distilled water is best because it is free from sodium. One or two glasses of mineral water should be fine, but you don't want to add excessive minerals to your body.

Promote bowel regularity by adding bulk to your diet. Whole bran is a good source for this. If constipated, take a natural laxative tea or preparation.

Flush the intestines gently. Do this in the following way: On the first day, mix three tablespoons of psyllium seeds in two ounces of juice and drink. Follow with a large glass of water. Do this three times that day. On the second day, mix three tablespoons of psyllium seeds in two ounces of juice and drink. Follow with a large glass of water. Do this two times that day. On the third day, mix three tablespoons of psyllium seeds in two ounces of juice and drink. Follow with a large glass of water. Do this one time.

If you break out from *insufficient digestive enzymes,* you may go to your local health food store and buy the needed enzymes. These are usually sold in the form of chewable tablets which are taken after meals. It might also be helpful to buy a bottle of acidopholis. This contains living bacteria naturally found in the intestines which aids in food digestion. Take three tablespoons before meals for one or two weeks. This is also an instant remedy for indigestion.

Part Four

THE MAKEUP OF MAKEUP

The Basics
of Bases

Up until a decade ago, makeup base or "foundation" was a thick, oily concoction, meant to be worn by "older women." When I began to experiment with makeup in my teens, my mother said, "Your skin is so lovely, why do you want to cover it up?" "Cover up" was what the old-fashioned bases were designed to do. It wasn't a natural look because none of the qualities of healthy, beautiful skin could show through.

Well, makeup bases have changed and so have the reasons to use them. The new bases are now available in hundreds of various "weights" from super sheer (light) to extra coverage (heavy). The most commonly found ones are mineral oil-based. But if you read the labels you will notice that there isn't a great deal of difference from one to another, yet they range in price from $5 to $50. I don't recommend these products because the mineral oil clogs pores, trapping toxins and preventing oxygen from reaching the skin. Oxygen is vital for the production of new cells, and trapped toxins can cause blemishes.

But don't trust the name of a product to tell you whether or not it is oil-free. One major cosmetic company (Clinique) makes a foundation called Water Base Makeup which, in fact, contains mineral oil. So, it's important to always read the ingredients label. The lightest bases, which give the least coverage, are water-based. The following are some recommended water-based foundations:

- Germaine Monteil's Clarity Water-base Face Color
- Clinique's Pore Minimizer Makeup
- Erno Laszlo's Shake It.

These water-based foundations are the ones that I recommend most frequently for the following reasons:

- They won't clog pores.
- They act as a protective barrier against mineral oil-based blushers, rouges, and highlighters.
- They act as a protective barrier against dirt and pollutants in the air and on our hands. Think of how many times a day you touch your face!
- They help to absorb excess oil as it is secreted.
- They even out skin tones and help to tone down or cover broken capillaries.
- They are undetectable. No one can tell that you're wearing "makeup."

Because of the protective functions of these bases, I recommend that all women past the age of 16 or 17 use them. The only exceptions would be teens or women with acne who may prefer to use a medicated base as prescribed by a dermatologist.

The type of base you choose is determined partially by skin type and partially by the purpose you want it to serve. All skin types could use the same water-based foundation, like Clinique or Laszlo; however, women with aging and/or dry skin usually prefer the look of an oil-based foundation. Oily skin types should never use an oil-based foundation because they want their base to help absorb their natural excess oil. The following natural oil-based foundations are recommended:

- Rachael Perry's Bee Pollen–jojoba Nutrient Makeup
- Germaine Monteil's Sport Tint
- Adrienne Arpel makes a glycerine-based foundation which serves the same purpose.

The way to assure a natural-looking base color is to choose one which matches your skin tone. That's why makeup manufacturers place "testers" on makeup counters. Just be sure to try the makeup on a clean face and check it in natural as well as artificial light. If you carry a small hand mirror with you to the store, you can apply the makeup, check it inside, then step outside to see how it looks in daylight. If it matches your coloring correctly, it will look good in any light.

I don't like testing for color on the back of the hands because very often the hands are darker than the face.

In the summer, if you like the look of a tan, you can choose a base which is one shade darker than your natural skin tone.

Following is a list of makeup bases recommended for each skin type. The letters (L), (M), and (H), indicate the amount of coverage. L = light, M = medium, and H = heavy.

If your skin type is **dry,** choose:
1. Laszlo's Shake It (L)
2. Clinique's Pore Minimizer Makeup (L)
3. Perscriptives Oil Free Foundation (L)

Since these are very light, water-based foundations, they give a matte finish which can emphasize fine lines. You may prefer the look of an oil-based foundation. If so, choose:
4. Germaine Monteil's Sport Tint (L)
5. Rachael Perry's Bee Pollen–jojoba Nutrient Makeup (H)
6. Adrienne Arpel's Liquid Powder (L)

If your skin type is **combination to the dry side** choose any of the above.

If your skin type is **oily** choose:
1. Laszlo's Shake It (L)
2. Clinique's Pore Minimizer Makeup (L)
3. Germaine Monteil's Water-base Face Color (L)
4. Elizabeth Arden's Oil Free Makeup (M)
5. Clientele Skin Tone Balancer (L)
6. Discipline Watercolor (L)

If your skin type is **combination to the oily side** choose any of the above.

If your skin is **aging** you'll need a moist, rich foundation to help the skin hold its natural moisture, and to minimize the appearance of fine lines. Unfortunately, there are only two foundations which I recommend in this category:

1. Rachael Perry's Bee Pollen–jojoba Nutrient Makeup (H)
2. Adrienne Arpel's Liquid Powder (L)

Basic Trimmings

Now that you know how to care for, protect, and nourish your skin, I want to give you some general information about makeup. The fact is that almost all compressed blushers, shadows, and powders—as well as pencils and lipsticks—contain mineral oil as a binder. But since you're going to be using protective products like aloe vera gel, natural oil-based moisturizer and foundation, or water-based foundation, you don't have to be too concerned about an undesirable ingredient, like mineral oil, touching your skin. It won't. Here are some tips to help you choose good basic trimmings.

Eye Shadow

Eye shadow comes in several forms.

Compressed eye shadows are powders usually held together with mineral oil or some other binder. They are applied with a brush or sponge applicator and some may also be moistened and used as eyeliner.

Powder eye shadows are loose, or loosely compressed. Both are applied with brushes. It is important to blow the excess from the brush before applying or it will fall on the cheeks. Women with drooping eyelids should not use this type of shadow because it will collect in the folds and creases of the eyelid.

Liquid eye shadows are creamy, and are packaged in a tube or wand, with a sponge-tipped applicator. These go on wet, then dry quickly and stay as applied until removed. Liquids are terrific for women with droopy lids and anyone else who likes shadow to stay put. They may also be used as eyeliner by using the side of the applicator, rather than the wide, broad surface. The only real differences between "five and dime" eye shadows and expensive ones are the choice of colors and the packaging. Both are significantly better in the more expensive products. Cheap shadow containers tend to fall apart quickly too.

Eyeliner

The two ways to use eyeliner are (1) to line the eyes as close to the lashes as possible with a thin line that looks as if it's part of the lashes, and (2) to line the eyes with a wide, soft line. For the first purpose use a color that matches the lashes or is one shade darker. For the second effect, any complimentary color may be used.

Cake liner is a hard, dry compact which must be moistened with water and applied with a fine brush. This type of liner lasts forever!

Liquid liner is a creamy liquid that comes in a tube, wand, or bottle, usually with its own brush applicator. I prefer the cake liners because they last longer and because you use your own brush with them. This means you can choose a high-quality brush and clean it carefully after each use. Once again, there is little or no difference from cheap to expensive liners, as far as chemical composition goes. You will have a better color choice in the more expensive lines.

Lipsticks

All lipsticks have basically the same wax base. However, they vary enormously, according to the amounts of emollients used. This is one case where price actually accounts for significant differences between products. Inexpensive lipsticks don't contain high-quality emollients. These substances condition the lips and help to prevent dryness. They also give the lipstick a creamy look. Cheap lipsticks "cake up" and can cause dryness. Very often they dry out or break in the tube. Revlon makes the best inexpensive lipsticks. Don't shop in the dime store for this product!

Blushers

Blushers are available in several different forms.

Loose powder blushers are my favorite form of blush, but they are not very convenient to use because they tend to spill easily. A small California-based company called Bare Essentials markets a line of these natural powders in an assortment of fantastic colors. Usually large health food stores or cosmetic boutiques will carry this line.

Pressed powder blushers conveniently come in compacts with a brush and a mirror, but they are all held together with mineral oil. As I mentioned earlier, if you're wearing aloe vera gel as toner and water-based makeup as base, you can safely use these blushers. Once again, there is little difference between expensive and cheap, except for color choice and packaging.

Liquid blushers are all mineral oil-based and will penetrate through makeup and aloe toner. I don't recommend their use.

Cream blushers have an even higher amount of mineral oil and seem to have a composition close to that of lipstick. Steer clear of these also.

Under Eye Concealers

These are available in several different forms, all of which are mineral oil-based.

Liquid (in tube or wand) are the best for everyday use because they are light and can be easily worked into the skin by lightly tapping with the finger tip. My favorite of these is made by Princess Marcella Borghese. It's called Eye Primer and Concealer, and is a two-sided wand, each with its own sponge applicator. One side is used under the eyes, and the other on the eyelids. This evens out the color on the lids and can be worn by itself or used as a base for eye shadow. It actually helps shadows to stay and gives a purer look to the color. The amount of mineral oil used in this product is very small.

Cream under eye concealers are small pots of thick concealer, made with lots of mineral oil and not recommended for use.

Stick concealer looks like a lipstick. Once again, the mineral oil content is too high and some form of wax is often used in these as well. It takes too much rubbing to blend this product also. I don't recommend these.

Something to remember when using under eye concealer is that light makes things protrude. So, only use concealer on the dark area in the corner or under the eye. If used on puffiness, it will emphasize it.

Mascara

I like the Bare Essentials and Redken mascara best because they contain no lacquer, won't smudge, and are easily removed. This type of mascara is becoming more popular and can be found in salons under various private labels in small makeup specialty shops.

There are several different brands of "waterproof" mascara which are good to use if you're going to swim or take a hot tub. However, don't use waterproof mascara all the time. It's too drying for your lashes. I don't like the mascaras that are classified as lash builders, because they contain fibers which have an irritating habit of flaking off, and can flake into your eyes. The good old cake-type mascaras, like Maybelline, are fine to use if you want to really build up your lashes. Simply apply one coat, let it dry, then apply one or two more.

There is little or no difference between cheap and expensive mascaras. The only real difference is whether or not they contain lacquer.

Soft Eye Crayons

The composition of eye crayons remains basically the same, regardless of price. The differences can be seen in color and texture. Expensive crayons have better colors, are easily applied, and will last longer. They also sharpen well, instead of falling apart.

Crayons do have a tendency to smudge on some people, like those with drooping eyelids, so try one at first to see how well you wear it. It helps to use the eye primer under these.

Pencils

These are used for eyebrows or to line the eyes. Once again, they're basically all the same except for color and texture. The expensive ones have a wider range of colors and emollients. Cheap pencils tend to be hard and will pull the delicate skin on the eyelid.

I know that an enormous amount of information has just been imparted to you. Please don't feel too overwhelmed. Take this book one step at a time, and make the routines part of your daily life. Before you know it, it will seem as if you've always taken care of your skin this way. The improvement will be immediate, and the effects will keep your skin healthy as well as beautiful.

Glossary of
Cosmetic Terms

Acetylated. Any organic compound that has been heated with acetic anhydride or acetyl chloride to remove its water. Acetylated lanolins are used in hand creams and lotions, for instance. Acetic anhydride produces irritation and necrosis of tissues in a vapor state and carries a warning against contact with skin and eyes.

Alkalai. The term originally covered the caustic and mild forms of potash and soda. Now a substance is regarded as an alkalai if it gives hydroxyl ions in solution. An alkaline aqueous solution is one with a pH greater than 7. Sodium bicarbonate is an example of an alkalai that is used to neutralize excess acidity in cosmetics.

Antioxidant. An agent such as Vitamin E that inhibits oxidation and thus prevents rancidity of oils or fats or the deterioration of other materials through exposure to oxygen.

Antiseptic. Germ killer.

Astringent. Usually promoted for oily skin. A clear liquid containing mostly alcohol, but with small amounts of other ingredients such as boric acid, alum, menthol, and/or camphor. In addition to making the skin feel refreshed, it usually gives a tightened feeling from the evaporation of the ingredients.

Dermatologist-tested. This indicates that the product has been tested for safety by one dermatologist. This does not necessarily indicate complete safety, effectiveness, or that the product is hypoallergenic.

Detergent. Any of a group of synthetic, organic, liquid, or water-soluble cleansing agents that, unlike soap, are not prepared from fats and oils and are not inactivated by hard water. Most of them are made from petroleum derivatives but vary widely in composition. The major advantage of detergents is that they do not leave a hard water scum. They also have wetting agent and emulsifying agent properties. Toxicity of detergents depends upon alkalinity. Dishwasher detergents, for instance, can be dangerously alkaline while detergents used in cosmetic products have an acidity-alkalinity ratio near that of normal skin.

Emollient. A substance or mixture of substances such as oils, which, when applied to skin, helps to prevent loss of moisture.

Emulsifier. Agents used to assist in the production of an emulsion. Among common emulsifiers in cosmetics are stearic acid soaps such as potassium and sodium stearates; sulfated alcohols such as sodium lauryl sulfate, polysorbates, poloxamers, and pegs; and sterols such as cholesterol.

Emulsion. What is formed when two or more nonmixable liquids are shaken so thoroughly together that the mixture appears to be homogenized. Most oils form emulsions with water.

Humectant. A substance added to another to help it retain moisture.

Hypoallergenic. "Hypo" means "less." So, hypoallergenic means less likely to cause allergic reaction.

Lubricant. Same as emollient.

Nonionic. A group of emulsifiers used in hand creams. They resist freezing and shrinkage.

Pearl Essence. Guanine. A suspension of crystalline guanine in nitrocellulose and solvents. Guanine is obtained from fish scales. No known toxicity to skin or nails.

Photosensitivity. A condition in which the application or ingestion of certain chemicals, such as propylparaben, causes skin problems, including rash, hyperpigmentation, and swelling, when the skin is exposed to sunlight.

Sensitizer. A substance which causes a reaction such as redness, itching or swelling, on the skin.

Sequestering Agent. A preservative, which prevents physical or chemical changes affecting color, flavor, texture, or appearance of a product. EDTA is an example. It prevents adverse effects of metals on shampoos.

Stabilizer. A substance added to a product to give it body and to maintain a desired texture, for instance, the stabilizer alginic acid, which is added to cosmetics.

Surfactant. A compound that makes it easier to effect contact between two surfaces; in cosmetics usually between the skin and a cream or lotion. A surfactant reduces surface tension, for example, such as lecithin does.

Wetting Agent. Any of numerous water-soluble agents that promote spreading of a liquid on a surface or penetration into a material such as skin. It lowers surface tension for better contact and absorption.

Cosmetic
Ingredient Dictionary

Ingredients found on labels of cosmetic products are listed alpha-
betically. Stars (☆) indicate the material is rated favorably, bullets
(•) indicate an unfavorable rating. Question marks (?) indicate that
the value of the ingredient has been challenged or that it can be a
potential danger to some persons.

- **Acetyl Ethyl Tetramethyl Tetralin (AETT):** A fixative or masking
  agent used in soap, aftershave and deodorants. It is absorbed through the skin and respiratory channels and
  causes internal organs to turn blue.

- **Activol** or **Aminophenol:** A photographic developer and an in-
  termediate in dyes used on furs and feathers.

☆ **Allantoin:** A natural compound occurring in tobacco seed,
  sugar beets, wheat sprouts, and the excretions of maggots.
  Soothing to the skin; may have a softening effect on dry
  skin.

☆ **Amyl dimethyl PABA:** Sunscreening agent.

- **Asbestos:** Sometimes found in talc. A proven carcinogen.

☆ **Avocado oil:** Obtained from the dehydrated sliced flesh of the
  avocado. An emollient.

☆ **Azulene:** An extract from the plant camomile. It is an anti-
  allergenic agent and soothing to the skin.

? **BHA:** Acts as preservative.

? *BHT:* Acts as an antioxidant.

? *Balsam:* Coats the hair each time it is used; this eventually becomes brittle and causes the hair to have a "lifeless quality," and break.

☆ *Benzaldehyde:* Artificial essential oil of almond.

☆ *Benzophenone-2:* Powder used in shampoos to keep light from fading the color of the shampoo.

☆ *Benzophenone-4:* Also used to protect color of shampoos; absorbs ultraviolet light.

☆ *Bismuth oxychloride:* Used as a pigment in cosmetics. A mildly astringent, antiseptic white powder.

• *Boric acid:* Sometimes used to pH balance shampoos. Should be avoided; penetrates skin rapidly and can poison.

• *2-Bromo-2-nitropropane-1, 3-diol:* Can form carcinogens in cosmetics or on the skin. Avoid products with this ingredient. Often in shampoos and moisturizers; sometimes called "BNPD."

☆ *Butylene glycol:* Used as a humectant (a substance added to another to help it retain moisture) in cosmetics; sweet odor.

? *Butylparaben:* A preservative.

☆ *Calcium carbonate:* Occurs naturally as limestone; excellent antacid.

☆ *Calcium silicate:* Anticaking agent.

? *Camphor:* Acts as a mild primary irritant to some persons and can be a contact allergen.

? *Candelilla wax:* A brittle solid used in lipsticks and creams.

? *Carbomer 934, 940, 941:* Used to form thick formulations in many cosmetics. Can cause eye irritation.

☆ *Carmine:* A natural pigment derived from the dried female insect coccus cacti; used as dye.

☆ *Carnauba:* From the Brazilian wax palm. Used in cosmetics such as depilatories and deodorant sticks.

☆ *Castor oil:* Used in cosmetic creams and other preparations (particularly lipstick) as an emollient and lubricant.

☆ *Cellulose gum:* Acts as an emulsifier and a thickener. Appears in shampoos as a suspending agent.

☆ *Ceresin:* White to yellow wax used as a substitute for beeswax.

☆ *Cetyl alcohol:* Used as an emollient, emulsion modifier, and coupling agent.

☆ *Cetyl lactate:* An emollient.

☆ *Cetyl palmitate:* Synthetic spermaceti.

☆ *Cholesterol:* Found in all body tissues. Acts as an emulsifying and lubricating agent in cosmetics.

☆ *Chromium hydroxide green:* A coloring agent.

☆ *Citric acid:* Found widely in plants and in animal tissues. Adjusts pH and acts as an antioxidant.

☆ *Cocamide DEA:* Acts as a foam stabilizer and thickener in shampoos.

? *Cocamide MEA:* Appears most often in shampoos; can be mildly irritating.

? *Cocoa butter:* It has emollient properties; frequently appears in suntan preparations. May produce contact sensitivities.

? *Coconut oil:* A saturated fat; the fat molecules are large, making the oil too "heavy" for facial skin.

? *D&C Green No. 4:* "Acid Green 25"; a coloring ingredient.

? *D&C Orange No. 5:* "Solvent Red 72"; can be toxic if ingested in large quantities; used in lipsticks, dentifrices, mouthwashes, etc.

? *D&C Orange No. 17 Lake:* An insoluble pigment found often in lipstick.

? *D&C Red No. 3 Aluminum Lake:* An insoluble pigment.

? *D&C Red No. 6 Barium Lake:* An insoluble pigment.

? *D&C Red No. 19:* "Basic Violet 10"; used in lipsticks, mouthwashes, etc.

? *D&C Red No. 21:* "Solvent Red 43"; a coloring.

? *D&C Red No. 33:* "Acid Red 33"; used in lipsticks, mouthwashes, etc.

• *D&C Yellow No. 10:* "Acid Yellow 3"; this dye could be contaminated with a carcinogen.

• *D&C Yellow No. 11:* "Solvent Yellow 33"; it is an allergen.

- *Diethanolamine (DEA):* May be contaminated.
- ☆ *Dimethicone:* A silicone-derived compound; skin protectant.
- ☆ *Ethylene Diamine Tetra Acetic Acid (EDTAA):* Used as a "complexing" agent in shampoos.
- ? *FD&C Blue No. 1 Aluminum Lake:* "Acid Blue No. 9"; a coloring.
- ? *FD&C Green No. 3:* A coloring.
- *FD&C Red No. 4:* A coloring no longer permitted for use.
- ? *FD&C Yellow No. 5:* "Acid yellow 23."
- ? *FD&C Yellow No. 5 Aluminum Lake:* A pigment.
- ☆ *Ferric ferrocyanide:* Used as pigment.
- *Fluorocarbons:* In aerosals, destroy ozone layer in atmosphere.
- ? *Formaldehyde:* Used in almost 1,000 cosmetics; a preservative. Possible animal carcinogen.
- ☆ *Glycerin:* Works as a humectant and emollient.
- ? *Glyceryl oleate:* Used as an emulsifier in lotions and creams. Eye contact may cause irritation.
- ☆ *Glyceryl stearate SE:* Used in shampoos as a pearlizing agent and as an emulsifier and opacifier in creams and lotions.
- *Hydrocarbons:* These are now under question.
- ☆ *Hydrolyzed animal protein:* Imparts a glossy sheen to hair.
- ☆ *Imidazolidinyl urea:* A preservative found in shampoos.
- ☆ *Iron oxides:* Used as pigment.
- ☆ *Isopropyl alcohol:* Dissolves oils; has antiseptic properties.
- ☆ *Isopropyl lanolate:* Acts as wetting agent for cosmetic pigments and is an emollient. Appears as a binder for pressed powders and as a lubricant in lipsticks.
- *Isopropyl myristate:* Used as an emollient and lubricant in pre-shaves, aftershaves, shampoos, bath oils, antiperspirants, deodorants, and various creams and lotions; causes skin irritation and clogs pores.
- ☆ *Isopropyl palmitate:* Used in many moisturizing creams. It easily penetrates the skin and also forms a thin layer on the skin.
- ☆ *Kaolin:* "China clay." Aids in absorption of oil and covering abil-

ity of face powders. Used in powders, foundations and facial masks.

☆ **Laneth-10 acetate:** Derived from lanolin. Acts as an emulsifier, a superfatting agent, and has some humectant properties.

? **Lanolin:** Found in hair conditioners, cream lotions, in lipsticks (as a binder) and in shampoos. Acts as an emulsifier; can cause allergic reactions. Used as a superfatting agent in soaps and shampoos.

☆ **Lanolin alcohol:** Used as a thickener for shampoos and bath gels. Gives many cosmetics a creamy texture and a high gloss.

? **Lanolin oil:** "Dewaxed Lanolin"; acts as a skin moisturizer and reduces stickiness of creams and lotions. Found also in hair conditioners, fingernail conditioners, and skin cosmetics.

☆ **Lauramide DEA:** Nonionic surfactant; builds and stabilizes foam in shampoos and bubble baths.

? **Laureth-23:** A nonionic surfactant found in shampoos.

☆ **Lecithin:** Found in living plants and animals. Lecithin has surfactant, emulsifier, and emollient properties.

☆ **Magnesium aluminum silicate:** Used as a thickener and stabilizer in cosmetic creams and shaving creams. It is a suspending agent and an antacid.

☆ **Magnesium carbonate:** Found in powders and covering preparations.

☆ **Magnesium silicate:** Used as an anticaking agent, opacifier and stabilizer.

☆ **Manganese violet:** A light violet powder; can be used around eyes.

? **Menthol:** An antiseptic and anesthetic and is found in skin lotions and shave creams. Has been shown to cause adverse reactions to users when in perfume or applied to skin in high concentrations.

? **Methylparaben:** Used as a preservative; a possible sensitizer and may cause allergic contact dermatitis.

☆ **Mica:** A naturally occurring mineral; imparts silkiness to powder products and acts as an opacifier.

☆ **Microcrystalline wax:** Used as stiffening and opacifying agent.

• **Mineral oil:** "Liquid Paraffin"; found in rouges, hand lotions, cold creams, and bath oils.

? **Montan wax:** Often used in place of carnauba wax.

• **Musk tetralin** and **Polycyclic musk:** A masking agent used in unscented deodorants. It causes nerve damage.

? **Octoxynol-1:** Used as an emulsifier and dispersing agent.

☆ **Octyl palmitate:** A yellowish solid used in creams and oils.

? **Oleic acid:** It is a common constituent of many animal and vegetable fats, and therefore of most normal diets. Used in cosmetics as an emollient in creams and lotions. Can be mildly irritating.

☆ **Oleyl alcohol:** Found in fish oils; softening and lubricating qualities.

☆ **Ozokerite:** Often used as a substitute for beeswax.

☆ **PEG-8:** A polymer of ethylene oxide. Acts as an emollient, plasticizer, and softener for cosmetic creams and shampoos.

• **PVM/MA copolymer:** Has thickening, dispersing and stabilizing properties; highly irritating to eyes, skin and mucous membranes.

☆ **PVP:** Forms a hard, transparent, lustrous film. Used primarily in hair sprays.

☆ **Panthenol:** Part of the water-soluble vitamin B complex. Used as an emollient and hair conditioner.

? **Para-aminobenzoic acid (PABA):** A sunscreening agent. Is not thought to be phototoxic or photoallergenic, but does have a weak potential for sensitization.

• **Parabens:** Preservatives and bacteria killers.

• **Paraffin:** Derived from petroleum. Used as a thickener for cosmetic creams.

• **Petrolatum:** "Petroleum Jelly"; appears in rouges, hand cleaners, lip pomades, hand lotions, lipsticks, and creams of all kinds.

? *Phenylmercuric acetate:* Used as a preservative in shampoos and eye cosmetics. It is highly toxic if inhaled or swallowed and can cause skin irritation.

☆ *Phosphoric acid:* Functions as a metal ion sequestrant and an acidifier.

☆ *Polysorbate-20:* Used as an emulsifier and solubilizer in many cosmetics and as an anti-irritant to reduce eye irritation in nonsting shampoos. Will reduce irritation of antiperspirants.

? *Propylene glycol:* Appearing in many cosmetics as a solvent and conditioning agent; has humectant properties. May cause allergic reaction in a small number of people.

☆ *Propylgallate:* Acts as an antioxidant (preservative).

☆ *Propylene glycol stearate:* Functions as an emollient, thickener, and emulsion stabilizer in creams and lotions.

• *Propylparaben:* A preservative widely used in cosmetics. A possible sensitizer.

• *Quaternium-15:* A preservative; a fairly potent sensitizer; accounts for a large number of cosmetic allergic reactions.

• *Quaternium-18:* Used as a conditioning agent in hair conditioners. It is an eye irritant and can cause contact dermatitis.

☆ *Quaternium-19:* A substantive (clinging) hair conditioner.

• *Resorcinol:* Is irritating to the skin and mucous membranes. Sometimes used as an antidandruff agent due to its antiseptic properties.

☆ *Silica:* Stabilizes emulsions and enhances flow of cosmetic powders. Will thicken cosmetic creams. *Caution:* Prolonged inhalation of dust may cause fibrosis of the lung.

☆ *Sodium borate:* A detergent builder, emulsifier, and preservative in cosmetics. *Caution:* Ingestion of 5 to 10 grams by young children can cause severe vomiting, diarrhea, and death.

• *Sodium hydroxide:* Found in oven and drain cleansers.

☆ *Sodium laureth sulfate:* Anionic (negatively charged) surfactant.

- **Sodium lauryl sulfate:** Used in many cosmetics as an emulsi-. fier and a detergent. Strongly degreases and dries skin.
? **Sodium sulfite:** Detergent builder, preservative, and antioxidant. Swells keratin.
☆ **Sorbic acid:** Made from berries of the mountain ash. A mold inhibitor and fungistatic agent. Also acts as a humectant in cosmetic creams and lotions.
☆ **Sorbitan laurate:** Used as an emulsifier in many cosmetics. Found to be nonirritating to eyes and skin.
☆ **Sorbitan sesquioleate:** An emulsifier; nonirritating to skin and eyes.
☆ **Sorbitan stearate:** An emulsifier; nonirritating to skin and eyes.
☆ **Sorbitol:** Used as a solvent for hair dyes. Gives holding properties to hair dressings. Humectant/emollient in polymer-type gels.
☆ **Stearalkonium chloride:** Extremely effective hair conditioner and softener.
☆ **Stearic acid:** Used in cosmetic creams to cut greasiness. A pearlizer in shampoos and lotions.
☆ **Stearyl alcohol:** Pearlizing agent, lubricant, and antifoam agent.
☆ **Squalene:** A bactericide and an emollient.
? **Talc:** Blocks of it are known as "soapstone"; adheres to skin and used as a filler in cosmetic creams to produce slip and coloring in powders. Depending on the source, some talcs may be contaminated.
? **TEA-lauryl sulfate:** High foaming agent. Prolonged skin contact may cause skin irritation.
? **Tetrasodium EDTA:** Sequestering agent; prolonged skin contact may cause irritation—even a mild burn.
☆ **Titanium dioxide:** Imparts whiteness, brightness, and opacity.
- **Toluenesulfonamide/formaldehyde resin:** Used as a plasticizer in nail polishes; a strong sensitizer.
- **Triclosan:** A bactericide with very high percutaneous absorption through intact skin. Can cause liver damage; is an eye irritant.

? **Triethanolamine (TEA):** An alkalizing agent in cosmetics.

☆ **Turkey red oil:** Used as a surfactant, emollient in cosmetic creams, skin cleansers, and bath oils.

☆ **Ultramarine blue:** Used as pigment.

☆ **Vitamin E:** The oil is too heavy to be used on the face on a daily basis. However, this makes an excellent ingredient in a weekly mask. It can also be used for healing cuts, abrasions and burns.

? **Wheat germ glycerides:** Derived by pressing wheat germ. A dietary source of vitamin E.

☆ **Zinc oxide:** Helps cosmetics adhere to skin and is widely used in powders and creams.

? **Zinc stearate:** Helps cosmetics adhere to skin and is widely used in powders and creams. May be harmful if inhaled.

ABOUT THE AUTHOR

Zia Wesley-Hosford came to the business of beauty via the Broadway stage. After appearing as a principle in the Broadway musicals "Hair" and "Godspell," she graduated from the Vidal Sassoon Academy in San Francisco. Since then she has worn the hats of beauty salon proprietor, fabric and clothes designer, exercise and dance instructor, cosmetologist, modeling teacher, and fine artist.

For the past eight years Zia has worked in the San Francisco Bay Area with thousands of clients on hair, skin, makeup, wardrobe, and figure design. She believes that, "It doesn't take more time or work to look better at forty than you did at twenty, it just takes know-how."